Compiled by Li Youyou

Translated by Shao Da

CHINESE CLAY SCULPTURES

CHINA INTERCONTINENTAL PRESS

图书在版编目（CIP）数据

中国民间泥塑：英文/李友友编著；邵达译.—北京：五洲传播出版社，2008.10
（中国民间工艺系列）
ISBN 978-7-5085-1313-3

Ⅰ.中…　Ⅱ.①李…②邵…　Ⅲ.泥塑－民间工艺－中国－英文
Ⅳ.J327

中国版本图书馆CIP数据核字（2008）第058023号

策　　划：荆孝敏
编　　著：李友友
顾　　问：李寸松
翻　　译：邵　达
特约编辑：吕　蕾
责任编辑：王　莉
装帧设计：缪　惟　林国霞

中国民间泥塑

出版发行：五洲传播出版社
社　　址：北京市海淀区莲花池东路北小马厂6号华天大厦
邮政编码：100038
电　　话：010-58891281
传　　真：010-58891281
制版单位：北京锦绣圣艺文化发展有限公司
印　　刷：北京郎翔印刷有限公司
开　　本：889x1194　1/24
印　　张：4.5
印　　数：1-3000册
版　　次：2009年10月第1版　2009年10月第1次印刷
书　　号：ISBN 978-7-5085-1313-3
06800（平）

Introduction

The art of clay figure modeling in China boasts a long history that dates back to the Neolithic Age (about 4,000 to 10,000 years B.P.). For instance, some pottery pigs and sheep have been discovered at the 6,000 to 7,000-year-old Hemudu site in Zhejiang Province. And the life-size terra cotta warriors and horses unearthed in 1974 from the mausoleum of the First Emperor (259-210 BC) of the Qin Dynasty (221-206 BC) have been referred to as the "Eighth Wonder of the Ancient World." In fact, archaeologists have excavated a great number of pottery figurines, animals, chariots, and boats from the tombs of the following Han Dynasty (206 BC-AD 220). Naturally, the funeral custom of burying figurines and objects with the dead gave impetus to the development of clay sculpture at that time.

The rise of Taoism and the introduction of Buddhism into China after the Han Dynasty led to the massive construction of Taoist and Buddhist temples, which needed the decoration of painted clay statues of Buddha and various Taoist immortals. Clay sculpture had its heyday during the Tang Dynasty (618-907), which was also a period when Buddhist statues were put up in large numbers in the Mogao Grottoes located in Dunhuang of northwest China's Gansu Province.

Ever since the Song Dynasty (960-1279) clay sculpture began to enter the secular sphere of life as people vied in buying clay oxen as a symbol to greet spring at the Beginning of Spring (usually falling on the 4th or 5th of February), or purchasing clay dolls named *mo-he-le* standing for the Herd-boy and the Weaving-girl on the seventh evening of the seventh lunar month when the two legendary lovers are supposed to meet[1]. As

---

[1] The Herd-boy and the Weaving-girl are two lovers in Chinese mythology, identified with the stars Altair and Vega, who are separated by the River of Heaven, or the Milky Way, and are permitted to meet only once a year, on the seventh day of the seventh lunar month when magpies form a bridge for them to pass over the barrier.

a result, the Ming (1368-1644) and Qing (1644-1911) dynasties witnessed a flourishing period of clay toy production and marketing, and clay craftsmen from Tianjin, Beijing, Huishan of Wuxi in Jiangsu Province, Fuyang of Chaozhou in Guangdong Province, and Junxian County in Henan Province, all enjoyed great prestige.

All clay sculptures roughly fall into three categories based on their social functions, namely, large statues enshrined in religious monasteries or ancestral halls, such as the Buddhist statues in the grottoes in Dunhuang and in the Maiji Mountains (also in Gansu Province), and the painted statues of imperial maids in the Song-Dynasty Jin Memorial Temple in Taiyuan of north China's Shanxi Province; small toys usually associated with various local folk customs; and indoor ornaments such as the colored clay figures made in Huishan of Wuxi and the decorative works by Zhang the clay-figurine master in Tianjin.

By and large, the widely-spread clay sculpture characterized by strong local features and styles is an important window to learn China's colorful folk arts and cultures.

【CONTENTS】

Painted Buddhist Statues in Dunhuang

The Mogao Grottoes located in Dunhuang of Gansu Province, whose construction began in 366 AD, contain 2,415 Buddhist sculptures in clay ranging from 30-meter giant statues to statuettes some dozen centimeters high, and spanning a period of 1,000 years. These statues of Buddha, Bodhisattvas, heavenly kings, arhats, and flying Apsaras are mostly sculptures-in-the-round, whilst some details such as clothing and ornaments were carved in low relief.

Almost as famous as the Buddhist sculptures are the colorful murals covering a total 45,000 square meters. Actually, the two match so well that they appear to have been designed for each other, thus creating a harmonious artistic ambience inside the caves.

Statue of a Bodhisattva
Late Tang Dynasty
Cave No. 196

Statue of a Bodhisattva
Mid-Tang Dynasty
Cave No. 127

Statue of a Heavenly King
Mid-Tang Dynasty
Cave No. 45

Statue of a Heavenly King
Mid-Tang Dynasty
Cave No. 384

5

Statue of a Bodhisattva
Western Wei Dynasty (535-556)
Cave No. 432

Statues of Maha Kassapa❶, a Bodhisattva, and a Heavenly King
Mid-Tang Dynasty
Cave No. 159

---

❶ Maha Kassapa is one of the chief disciples of Buddha.

7

Flying Apsaras
Northern Wei
Dynasty (386-534)
Cave No. 437

8

Statue of Buddha
Mid-Tang Dynasty
Cave No. 319

Clay Sculptures in Beijing

Legend has it that in the 20th year of Guangxu (1894), a Peking Opera lover surnamed Gui began to draw facial make-up in operas on clay masks, which were called the "Gui flowery faces[1]." After the Revolution of 1911 that overthrew the Qing Dynasty, the production of clay masks with facial make-up gradually developed into a popular industry in Beijing.

Other traditional clay sculptures produced in the old capital city include the rabbit god (*tu-ye*), a toy played by children at the Mid-Autumn Festival, and the sword-and-horse figurines portraying various people on horseback (thus the name) and showing the local conditions and customs here.

---

[1] The flowery-face or *jing* role in Peking Opera represents a man of virile or rough character, singing and speaking in a full raucous voice rising to protracted enunciation of tremendous volume.

Clay Mask with Facial Make-up in Peking Opera
The Republic of China (1912-1949)

Clay Mask with Facial Make-up in Peking Opera
The Republic of China (1912-1949)

Clay Mask with Facial Make-up in Peking Opera
The Republic of China (1912-1949)

Clay Mask with Facial Make-up in Peking Opera
The Republic of China (1912-1949)

The Rabbit God Riding a Deer
In the collection of the Imperial Palace Museum of Beijing

Lady Chang'e is the Chinese moon goddess figuring prominently in legend and literature, who in mortal life swallows an elixir stolen from her husband and flies to the moon, where she becomes immortal but has been cloistered forever. Accompanying her in the Lunar Palace is a Jade Hare (Rabbit God) that keeps pounding cure-all medicine in a mortar. As early as in the Ming Dynasty, people began to enshrine and worship the rabbit god (or *tu-ye* in Chinese) at the Moon Festival (also known as the Mid-Autumn Festival falling on the 15th day of the eighth lunar month), in the hope to prevent disease and ward off disasters. Later on the clay-molded rabbit god in human shape, usually riding a deer, tiger or *kylin* (an auspicious legendary unicorn), or sitting on a lotus throne, became a popular children's toy for the festive occasion.

The Rabbit God
Made by Shuang Qixiang

The Rabbit God Riding a Tiger
Made by Shuang Qixiang

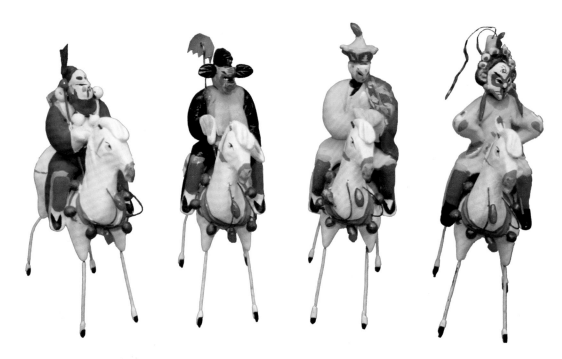

Sword-and-Horse Figurines: The Tang Monk and His Disciples[1]
Made by Han Baocai

[1] The Tang Monk and his disciples Monkey King, Pigsy, and Friar Sand are the four main characters in the classical novel entitled *Pilgrimage to the West* by Wu Cheng'en of the Ming Dynasty.

Sword-and-Horse Figurines:
A Princess Consort Going Downtown
Made by Han Zengqi

Sword-and-Horse Figurines:
A Horse-drawn Covered Carriage
Made by Han Zengqi

A Baby Girl Holding a Carp
Made by Shuang Qixiang

A Baby Boy Holding a Carp
Made by Shuang Qixiang

Traditionally, the fish has many auspicious implications. It is homophonic to the word of "superfluity" (*yu*) in Chinese language. There is a folk legend of "carp leaping over the dragon's gate," suggesting that a candidate succeeds in the ancient imperial civil examination and then a rewarding official career is ahead. What's more, the carp that can spawn tens of thousands of eggs has been regarded as the symbol of high fertility. Therefore, the sculpture of "a baby holding a carp" expresses people's wish to have more offspring and to live a life of affluence.

Ox Baby
Made by Shuang Qixiang

Tiger Baby
Made by Shuang Qixiang

According to the *General Customs* by Ying Shao of the Eastern Han Dynasty (25-220), the tiger is the king of all animals that can swallow up ghosts and goblins. Therefore, it has been worshipped as a protecting deity supposed to exorcise evil spirits.

**Golden Monkeys Offering
Peaches of Immortality
Made by Zhou Chongshan**

Pigsy Beating a Wooden Fish

Pigsy is a character in the novel *Pilgrimage to the West*, known for his laziness and stupidity. The wooden fish is a percussion instrument made of a hollow wooden block, originally used by Buddhist monks to beat rhythm when chanting scriptures.

Works by Zhang the Clay-figurine Master of Tianjin

Zhang Changlin (1826-1906), styled Mingshan, who was born in Tianjin in the late Qing Dynasty, learned from his father the art of molding clay figurines since childhood, and got the name of "Zhang the clay-figurine master" at the age of 18. His painted sculpture of a "Weaving Girl" won a first prize at the 1915 Panama Pacific International Exposition held in San Francisco. After the founding of the People's Republic in 1949, a "Clay Figurine Master Zhang's Studio" was set up in Tianjin; and inherited and further developed by Zhang Changlin's offspring (including Zhang Yuting, Zhang Jingfu, Zhang Jingxi, Zhang Jinghu, and Zhang Ming), the craft gradually spread to north China and formed its unique artistic style. Those clay figurines range from historical and theatrical characters to all kinds of unimportant persons, thus reflecting a vast spectrum of social life.

Heavenly Empress
Made by Lu Tong

Mazu, also known as Heavenly Empress in Taoist mythology, was born in a fisherman's family in Putian of Fujian Province. Her mortal name of Lin Moniang (meaning "silent girl") comes from a fairy tale that she didn't cry within a month after birth. Legend has it that with the blessing of Guanyin (the Goddess of Mercy in Buddhism), she once saved her father and brothers who went fishing on the sea from a typhoon. After her death at the age of 28, she became the goddess of the sea; and ever since the Ming and Qing dynasties Mazu temples have been built all over the coastal areas of southeast China.

An Old Man Scratching His Foot
Made in the Qing Dynasty, in the collection of
the Imperial Palace Museum of Beijing

Wang Zhaojun
Made by the Clay Figurine Master Zhang's Studio

Wang Zhaojun, ranked among the "Four Great Beauties" of ancient China, was a lady-in-waiting at the Western Han (206 BC-AD 25) imperial court who volunteered to marry the chief of the Huns in 33 BC, and thus helped to strengthen the dynasty's friendly ties with kingdoms of the Western Regions that included what's now Xinjiang and parts of Central Asia.

Diao Chan
Made by the Clay Figurine Master Zhang's
Studio

Diao Chan, one of the "Four Great Beauties" of ancient China, was a fictional character in the classical novel entitled *Romance of the Three Kingdoms* by Luo Guanzhong of the early Ming Dynasty.

A Baby
Made by Yang Zhizhong from the Clay Figurine Master Zhang's Studio

Playing the Game of Hawk and Chicks
Made by Yang Zhizhong from the Clay Figurine Master Zhang's Studio

Doing a *Yang-ge* Dance
Made by Yang Zhizhong from the Clay Figurine Master Zhang's Studio
Yang-ge is a very popular form of Chinese folk dance handed down from antiquity.

May All Go Well with You
Made by the Clay Figurine Master Zhang's Studio

Maternal Affection
Made by Yang Zhizhong from the Clay Figurine Master Zhang's Studio

A Bridegroom and a Bride
Made by Yang Zhizhong
from the Clay Figurine
Master Zhang's Studio

A Carefree Old Man
Made by Zhang Yusheng from the Clay Figurine Master Zhang's Studio

Laozi Going West from the Hangu Pass
Made by Zhang Yusheng from the Clay Figurine Master Zhang's Studio

Laozi was the reverent term of address for Li Er, who was a famous philosopher of the late Spring and Autumn Period. Later he was revered as the founder of Taoism. Originally he worked as a historiographer in charge of the archives for the royal court of Zhou❶. Noting the dynasty was slowly falling into decay, one day he left for the west via the Hangu Pass (located in the present Lingbao County of Henan Province) to live in seclusion. Tradition has it that Yin Xi, an official in charge of the defense of the Sanguan Pass (located in the present Baoji City of Shaanxi Province), saw the purple air coming from the east -- presumably a propitious omen, and thus predicted that a sage would appear. Laozi riding a buffalo soon showed up just as expected; Yin Xi asked him to write the *Classic of the Way and Virtue* (the main classic of Taoism) there before joining him on the journey to the west.

❶ The Zhou Dynasty in ancient China was divided into the Western Zhou (c. 1100-771 BC) and the Eastern Zhou, whilst the Eastern Zhou was further divided into the Spring and Autumn Period (770-476 BC) and the Warring States Period (475-221 BC).

Infusing a Bowl of Seasoned Flour Mush
Made by the Clay Figurine Master Zhang's Studio

The seasoned flour mush is made by stirring flour with boiling water and served with pepper, salt and sesame butter.

All Trades and Professions: A Cobbler
Made by the Clay Figurine Master Zhang's Studio

Zhong Kui Catching a Ghost
Made by the Clay Figurine Master Zhang's Studio

According to folk legend, in the early Tang Dynasty Zhong Kui from Mount Zhongnan went to the capital city of Chang'an (the present Xi'an in Shaanxi Province) to take part in the imperial civil examination, and came out first. However, at the final palace exam the treacherous Prime Minister Lu Qi who judged people by appearances stripped him of the title of "Number One Scholar" (or *zhuang-yuan* in Chinese) for he looked rather ugly. Feeling extremely ashamed and indignant, Zhong Kui killed himself by bumping his head against the palace column. After his death, Jade Emperor of Heaven (the supreme god of Taoism) made him the deity of driving away demons. Once Emperor Xuanzong (685-762) of the Tang dreamed that Zhong Kui caught and swallowed a ghost in the palace. When he awoke, the emperor ordered court painter Wu Daozi to draw a portrait of the demon-chaser. It had ever since become a tradition to paste Zhong Kui's pictures as charms at the entrance to houses to ward off evil influences.

Clay Sculptures in Hebei Province

The clay sculpture in Baigou, Yutian and Xincheng of north China's Hebei Province features a bold and unsophisticated style. Folk artisans often paint clay idols (molded into theatrical characters or auspicious animals) white at first, and then sketch details on it with red, green, black, blue or yellow. The multicolored images on a white background are very eye-catching.

Return to Parents' Home for a Visit After Marriage
Made in Baigou

The *Kylin* Bringing a Baby
Made in Yutian

The *kylin* is an auspicious legendary unicorn with scales all over its body. Chinese people used to believe that by worshipping it in all sincerity, they might be able to have a baby soon.

Mu Guiying in Command
Made in Yutian

The heroine in China's traditional opera entitled *Female Generals of the Yang Family*, Mu Guiying is the granddaughter-in-law of Yang Ye (also known as Yang Jiye) -- a famous general of the Northern Song Dynasty (960-1127). After most male members of the general's family were killed on the battlefield, Mu Guiying took over the seal of a commander-in-chief and defeated the invading Tanguts from the northwest.

Chen Shimei
Made in Yutian

Chen Shimei, a notorious character in traditional Chinese opera, is now a derisive title for a person who abandons his wife and seeks new romance with the elevation of his position.

A Character in the *Romance of the Three Kingdoms*: Cao Cao
Made in Yutian

A military strategist, statesman and writer during the last years of the Eastern Han Dynasty, Cao Cao (155-220) was notorious for his treachery in Chinese history. His son Cao Pi (187-226) established in 220 the State of Wei, one of the Three Kingdoms (220-280) covering today's provinces in the Yellow River valley and Hubei, Anhui, northern Jiangsu and central Liaoning.

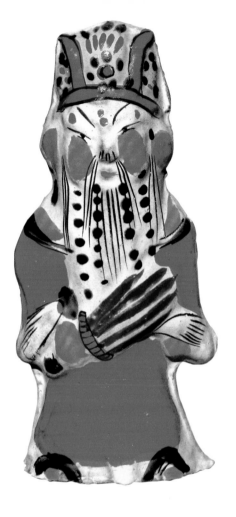

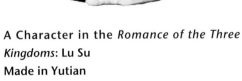

A Character in the *Romance of the Three Kingdoms*: Zhuge Liang
Made in Yutian

Zhuge Liang (181-234), styled Kongming, was a famous military strategist and statesman in the State of Shu (located roughly in the present Sichuan Province) during the period of the Three Kingdoms, who later became an incarnation of wisdom and resourcefulness in Chinese folklore.

A Character in the *Romance of the Three Kingdoms*: Lu Su
Made in Yutian

Lu Su (172-217), styled Zijing, was a military strategist and statesman in the State of Wu (embracing the middle and lower reaches of the Yangtze River) during the period of the Three Kingdoms.

A Roly-poly
Made in Baigou

Often painted in the images of a baby, an old man, or an ugly official, it's a self-righting doll very popular with children.

A Rooster
Made in Baigou

According to folk legend, the rooster, a harbinger of dawn, can exorcise evil spirits. What's more, the rooster is homophonic to the word of "good luck" (*ji*) in Chinese language, and thus it has become an auspicious image in Chinese culture.

Two Kittens
Made in Baigou

Clay Sculptures in Henan Province

The counties of Junxian and Huaiyang are two major areas manufacturing clay dolls in central China's Henan Province.

The Weihe River flows southwards through Junxian County located in northern Henan. The painted clay dolls here -- often molded into the shape of warriors on horseback, Monkey King, Pigsy and various animals -- are called *ni-gu-gu* in local dialect. Legend has it that in the Sui Dynasty (581-618), after capturing Liyang (ancient name of Junxian) the insurrectionary Wagang Army molded clay figurines to grieve for the officers and soldiers killed in action; the custom has been handed down to this very day. On the 15th day of the first and the seventh lunar month, local women go to the temple fair to buy *ni-gu-gu*, and when returning home by boat, throw the dolls to children singing and playing on the riverbank; it's a folk tradition to pray for a baby born into their own families.

Huaiyang, known as Wanqiu or Chenzhou in ancient times, is where Fuxi and Nüwa created human beings in Chinese mythology. Every year from the second day of the second lunar month to the third day of the third lunar month, a grand temple fair is held here to commemorate the two human ancestors. The clay dolls sold in the marketplace -- often painted on a black background and molded into the shape of various strange birds and animals -- are called *ni-ni-gou* in local dialect. Devout men and women vie in buying them in the hope of warding off evils and praying for good fortune.

48

Twelve Symbolic Animals
Made by Wang Lantian from Junxian County

According to the ancient custom, a total of twelve symbolic animals (namely, the rat, ox, tiger, rabbit, dragon, snake, horse, sheep, monkey, rooster, dog, and pig) are associated with a twelve-year cycle to respectively denote the year of a person's birth; they are called *sheng-xiao* or *shu-xiang* in Chinese language. People believe that these animals can bring peace, happiness and good luck to them.

Unicorn
Made in Junxian County

The unicorn, also called *xie-zhi* in Chinese, is a legendary animal credited with the ability to distinguish between right and wrong, virtue and evil. In ancient times, its image was embroidered on the front of the ceremonial gown worn by supervisory officials to symbolize justice. In the eyes of ordinary people, the unicorn is both a chaser of demons and a guardian spirit that watches over children.

A Lion Playing with a Colored Silk Ball
Made in Junxian County

A homophone for the Grand Duke (or *tai-shi*, the highest-ranking official to assist a king in managing state affairs in ancient times), the fierce lion (*shi*) has been regarded as an auspicious animal to expel evil spirits and bring blessings. Tradition also has it that by playing with a silk ball which is homophonic to the word of "praying" (*qiu*) in Chinese, a lioness may get pregnant and give birth to her cubs; therefore, the clay sculpture signifies a family of many children. What's more, the lion dance is a very popular folk dance performed on lunar New Year's Day or other festivals.

Unicorn
Made in Junxian County

A Battle Steed
Made in Junxian County

Located by the old course of the Yellow River, Junxian County -- a granary in the Central Plains -- has been a place of strategic importance since ancient times. After capturing it the Wagang Army that rose against the Sui Dynasty molded warriors and horses in clay to grieve for their fellow soldiers killed in action. Ever since then clay horses in various postures have been the most representative of the *ni-gu-gu* sculptures produced here.

53

Fierce Animals
Made in Junxian County

A Couple of Sheep
Made in Junxian County

A Tiger's Head
Made in Junxian County

Characters in the *Romance of the Three Kingdoms*: Cao Cao and Lord Guan
Made in Junxian County

Lord Guan is the reverent term of address for Guan Yu (160-219), a famous general of Shu of the Three Kingdoms. In the last years of the Eastern Han Dynasty, Guan Yu, Zhang Fei and Liu Bei (161-223, founder of the State of Shu) became sworn brothers. When defeated in Xiapi (the present Pixian County of Jiangsu Province), Guan temporarily surrendered to Cao Cao, but left escorting his sisters-in-law as soon as hearing the news of Liu Bei. He thus became an incarnation of loyalty and righteousness in Chinese folklore.

Dragon
Made in Huaiyang County

One of the twelve symbolic animals, the dragon has been the symbol of the emperor in China. Dragon worship is a very important element in Chinese culture, and Chinese people usually call themselves the offspring of the dragon.

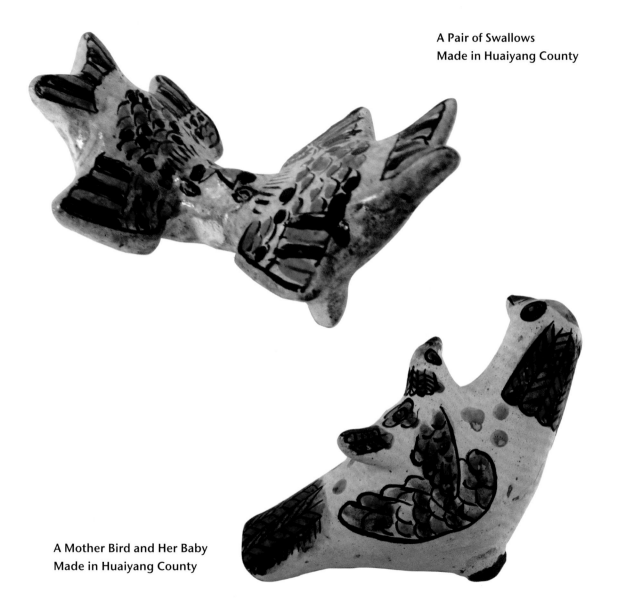

A Pair of Swallows
Made in Huaiyang County

A Mother Bird and Her Baby
Made in Huaiyang County

59

A Monkey
Made by Shao Bo

Monkey the Human Ancestor
Made in Huaiyang County

Monkey the Human Ancestor, mainly made in the villages near Taihao Mausoleum -- Fuxi's resting place, is the representative work of Huaiyang's *ni-ni-gou* sculptures. In Chinese mythology Fuxi and Nüwa have sexual intercourse and then have human beings. The patterns painted on the figurine symbolize female genitals, and reveal the ancient people's mysterious reproduction-worship cults. It has thus been regarded as the "living fossil" of Chinese folk art.

Strange Animal
Made in Huaiyang County

Unicorn
Made in Huaiyang County

Strange Animal
Made by Shao Bo from Huaiyang County

Clay Sculptures in Fengxiang of Shaanxi Province

Clay sculpture is closely related to a wide variety of folk activities in Fengxiang County of northwest China's Shaanxi Province. On the 10th day of the fourth lunar month every year, a temple fair is held on Mount Lingjiu some 15 kilometers west of the county town to worship the Old Lady, a deity in local myths. The custom allegedly originated from the Ming Dynasty. Devout believers go to the fair from all directions to offer sacrifices to the goddess, whilst buying clay toys in the shape of various animals such as lions, tigers, horses, cattle and sheep to pray for good fortune and babies. Of the figurines sold in the market-place, the sitting tiger as a house guardian and the tiger mask are probably the most popular, as the tiger has been regarded by local people as an auspicious animal supposed to repel evil spirits and avert misfortunes.

Colored Tiger Mask
Made by Hu Xinpeng

Local people of Fengxiang have the tradition to buy a tiger mask and hang it at home on the lunar New Year's Eve, in the hope of averting calamities and bringing blessings. Colorful auspicious patterns of peony and lotus flowers and pomegranates are painted on the mask which is made of clay and paper pulp and covered with a coat of varnish.

Black-and-white Tiger Mask
Made by Hu Xinpeng

Simply sketched in black and white, this unvarnished tiger mask is equally awe-inspiring.

Sitting Tiger
Made by Hu Xinpeng

The sitting tiger as a house guardian to expel evil spirits and bring good fortune is the representative work of Fengxiang's clay sculptures. It's usually displayed at home on lunar New Year's Day or other festivals, and the auspicious designs of peony, pomegranate, Buddha's-hand and calabash on its body painted in gorgeous colors such as bright red, green and yellow produce a strong decorative effect and convey to people a feeling of jubilation and celebration.

A Sheep Mask
Made by Hu Xinpeng

"With three *yang* begins prosperity" (*san yang kai tai*) is an auspicious expression used on lunar New Year's Eve to wish a good year to come. It comes from the *tai* hexagram[1] of the *Book of Changes* (one of Confucian classics), which in calendrical lore is correlated with the first month and whose three unbroken lines, underneath three broken ones, are three strokes of *yang* (positive force) -- a homophone for the word of sheep in Chinese language.

---

[1] ䷊ *tai* hexagram - the symbol of prosperity

A Horse
Made by Hu Shen

An Ox
Made by Hu Xinpeng

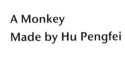

A Monkey
Made by Hu Pengfei

A Rabbit
Made by Hu Xinpeng

A Toad
Made by Hu Xinpeng

    Legend has it that there is a three-legged toad living in the moon, and a golden crow in the sun; they thus become the symbol of the two celestial bodies separately in Chinese mythology.

Liu Hai Playing with a Golden Toad
Made by Hu Pengfei

Liu Hai, also known by his literary name Haichanzi, is a Taoist immortal, and the three-legged golden toad is a magical animal in Chinese folklore. This clay sculpture has an implication of good luck and great prosperity.

A Pig

Once a totem worshipped by ancient people, the pig has been regarded as the symbol of bumper harvest and wealth in Chinese society. What's more, pigs, cattle and sheep are the three domestic animals used as sacrificial offerings in ancient times.

A Rooster
Made by Hu Xinpeng

Two Lions
Made by Hu Xinpeng

The God of Wealth
Made by Hu Pengfei

The Sworn Brotherhood of the Three Shu Heroes in the Peach Garden

Liu Bei, Guan Yu and Zhang Fei, three characters in the *Romance of the Three Kingdoms*, became sworn brothers and together established the State of Shu.

Clay Sculptures in Shandong Province

Niejia Village in Gaomi City is noted in east China's Shandong Province for its clay sculptures. According to the genealogical book of the Nie family, a person named Nie Fulai began to mold clay figurines as early as in the reign of Emperor Wanli (1573-1620) of the Ming Dynasty; it gradually became a household industry in the village by the period of Emperor Kangxi (1662-1722) of the Qing Dynasty, and had its heyday during the reign of Emperor Qiaqing (1796-1820) when clay whistles in the shape of animals such as tigers, lions, monkeys and roosters were made in batches. The clay figurines produced in Jinan, Linyi and Cangxian County in the province are also known far and wide.

**Toy Whistle in the Shape of a Tiger
Made in Niejia Village**

The front and rear part of the clay tiger are molded separately, and are joined together by parchment with a small whistle put in between. When being pressed, the tiger will whistle through its opening mouth.

A Pair of Lions
Made in Niejia Village

Toy Whistle in the Shape of a Lion
Made in Niejia Village

Rabbit King
Made by Zhou Jingfu from Jinan

According to folk legend, an infectious disease once spread in Jinan, the capital of Shandong Province. At the Mid-Autumn Festival a man named Ren Han sneaked into the Lunar Palace to steal the magic drug from the Moon Goddess. With the help of the Jade Hare pounding medicine in a mortar there, he safely returned to earth, and put the remedies into the 72 springs in the city. After drinking the spring water all patients recovered from the illness, and since then a tradition has been set for local people to mold rabbits in clay to commemorate the kind-hearted Jade Hare.

A Baby Holding a Fish
Made in Gaomi

A Buffalo Boy
Made in Gaomi City

Theatrical Characters

Liu Hai Playing with a Golden Toad
Made in Gaomi

The Eight Immortals

In Taoist mythology, on her legendary birthday (the third day of the lunar third month) the Queen Mother of the West dwelling at Jasper Lake in the Kunlun Mountains invites various immortals to come to taste the peaches of longevity grown in her palace. Once on their way back from the yearly grand gathering, the Eight Immortals -- usually identified as Han Zhongli, Zhang Guolao, Han Xiangzi, Li Tieguai, Lü Dongbin, Cao Guojiu, Lan Caihe, and He Xiangu -- choose to cross the eastern seas, each displaying his or her magic power.

Huishan Clay Figurines

There are accounts of Huishan clay figurines in historical records of the Ming Dynasty. The town of Huishan is located in the western outskirts of Wuxi, Jiangsu Province, and clay sculpture here was at its zenith in the middle period of the Qing Dynasty. Emperor Qianlong (1711-1799) allegedly gasped with admiration at the superb skill of local artisan Wang Chunlin during his inspection tour to south China. Huishan clay figurines roughly fall into two categories: children's toys like the doll of A-fu, and sculptures of theatrical characters. Local people have the tradition to buy these exquisite handicrafts when strolling around a temple fair, going together on a pilgrimage mission, going for an outing in early spring, or sweeping the ancestral graves (a ceremony to pay respects to the dead) at the Qingming Festival that usually falls on the fifth or sixth of April.

A Lucky Baby Girl
Made by Liu Chengyin

A Little Girl Wearing Flowers in Her Hair
Made by Wang Guodong

A-fu
Made by Yu Xianglian and Wang Nanxian

Legend has it that fierce animals and snakes were rampant in Huishan in ancient times; fortunately, a virgin boy descending from heaven exterminated all those evil creatures. In commemoration of the savior, folk artisans made a clay doll and gave it an auspicious name of A-fu (meaning "good fortune" in Chinese). Since then the figurine has become the mascot for the local people.

All Trades and Professions: A Peddler Selling Live Fowls

All Trades and Professions: A Doll Seller

All Trades and Professions: A Bricklayer

rades and Professions: A Monkey Show

Theatrical Characters: Liang Shanbo and Zhu Yingtai

Made by Chen Ronggen

The legend of "Butterfly Lovers" tells the romantic story of Liang Shanbo and Zhu Yingtai presumably living in the Eastern Jin Dynasty (317-420). Zhu Yingtai, a beautiful, intelligent young girl, disguises herself as a man so as to go to Hangzhou City to study at an academy of classical learning there. On the way to Hangzhou she encounters Liang Shanbo and they become "sworn brothers". After studying together for three years, Shanbo knows Yingtai's true gender at last and the two naturally fall in deep love with each other. Unfortunately, the romance ends up with a tragedy: Shanbo and Yingtai are unable to get married during their lifetime but can only be buried in the same grave after death. However, a pair of butterflies fly out of their tomb, indicating that the two lovers will never be separated again.

Characters in the *Female Generals of the Yang Family* Made by Chen Ronggen

Two Characters in the *Romance of the Three Kingdoms*: Mi Heng and Cao Cao
Made by Chen Ronggen

In the last years of the Eastern Han Dynasty, Chief of Beihai Prefecture Kong Rong (Confucius's descendant in the 20th generation) recommended Mi Heng, a person with a literary reputation, to Chief Minister Cao Cao. However, Cao only used him as a drumbeater. Refusing to take his humiliation lying down, Mi gave a good scolding to Cao in the presence of all the ministers and generals of the imperial court.

Clay Sculptures in Other Places

Other places in China that produce clay sculptures include Xinjiang Uygur Autonomous Region, Liupanshan of Ningxia Hui Autonomous Region, Qingyang of Gansu Province, Luochuan of Shaanxi Province, and Chaozhou of Guangdong Province.

The clay figurines of Xinjiang, simply painted white or black, reveal a kind of crude primeval beauty. The Yang family in Liupanshan has made clay sculptures for six generations; though primitive in form, their works -- either religious statues or indoor ornaments -- have very high artistic value. The lines of the clay animals made in Qingyang are simple and graceful; besides, they are often painted in rich colors, creating a strong visual effect. Yang Meiying from Luochuan is a female artisan known for her maternity-themed sculptures. The Wu family in Chaozhou is another old family as famous as the Zhang in Tianjin and the Yang in Ningxia, boasting a 700-odd-year history of molding clay figurines. Various toys and sculptures of theatrical characters produced here suggest that they have been under some kind of influence from Huishan of Wuxi.

The Twin Genii He-He
Made by the Wu family in Chaozhou of Guangdong

Legend has it that Han-shan and Shi-de had been as close as blood-brothers, but fell in love with a same girl without knowing it. Learning the truth just before marrying the girl, Han-shan then went to Suzhou to become a monk. Shi-de also left home to join his friend, and they together established the Hanshan Temple there. The two close friends have ever since been revered as the twin genii He-He, namely, the gods of harmonious union. Their pictures, one holding a lotus flower and the other a round box, used to be displayed at wedding ceremonies.

A Bird
Qingyang, Gansu

Wang Maosheng Offering a Jar of "Wine"
Made by the Wu family in Chaozhou of Guangdong

The sculpture is based on a same-titled Chaozhou opera popular in eastern Guangdong, southern Fujian and Taiwan. Xue Rengui, a famous general of the Tang Dynasty, once makes a triumphal return to his native place and gives a banquet in honor of guests. His past-time friend Wang Maosheng is invited. However, Wang is too poor to buy any gifts; so he and his wife carry a jar of water falsely claiming that it's wine. Xue does not nail the lie to embarrass Wang, and his benevolence and generosity have become a favorite topic among the people.

The Deity of Horse
Made by the Yang family in
Liupanshui of Ningxia

The Deity of Pig
Made by the Yang family in
Liupanshui of Ningxia

An Old Uygur Man
Xinjiang

A Clay Jar of Life
Made by Yang Meiying from Luochuan of Shaanxi

Breastfeeding a Baby
Made by Yang Meiying from Luochuan of Shaanxi

References

A Dictionary of Chinese Folk Art by Zhang Daoyi, Jiangsu Fine Arts Publishing House, Nanjing, 2001;

Collected Works of Chinese Folk Art: Toys by Li Cunsong, Zhejiang People's Fine Arts Publishing House, Hangzhou, 2002;

A Brief Introduction to Chinese Folk Toys by Wang Lianhai, Beijing Industrial Art Publishing House, 1991;

Chinese Folk Painted Sculptures by Zhang Chang and Zhang Hongyue, Hebei Children's Publishing House, Shijiazhuang, 2007.